# FAITH BASED INVESTING:

## Seven Biblical Rules For Investing

## D. ANTHONY WRIGHT

# CONTENTS

# REGULATORY ISSUES

This publication contains the opinions and ideas of its author. The strategies outlined in this book may not be suitable for every individual and are not guaranteed or warranted to produce any particular results. The author is an ordained minister and an Investment Advisor Representative. Investment advisory services are offered through Optivise Advisory Services, LLC a SEC registered investment advisor.

Presentations of performance data herein does not imply that similar results will be achieved in the future. Any such data are provided merely for illustrative and discussion purposes rather than focusing on the time periods used or the results derived. The reader shall focus instead on the underlying principles.

This book is sold with the understanding that neither publisher nor author through this book is engaged in rendering legal advice, tax advice, investment, insurance, financial, accounting, or any other professional advice or services. If the reader requires such advice or services, a competent professional should be consulted. Relevant laws vary from state to state.

No warranty is made with respect to the accuracy or the completeness of the information contained herein, and both the author and the publisher specifically disclaim any responsibility for any liability, loss, or risk, personal or otherwise, that is incurred as a consequence, directly or indirectly, of the use and application of any of the contents of this book.

Lastly, this book is written under the right of the First Amendment to the Constitution of the United States. This book is written as an outside business activity from my investment, advisory, and securities business.

Hello! I am Anthony Wright, CEO of Faith In The Word, World Wide Ministries, Inc. I am also CEO of Retirement Specialty Group, Inc., an investment firm with the Corporate office in Cookeville, Tennessee.

You may know me as the host of a syndicated financial radio show on one of many local radio stations in Tennessee, including my nationwide Sirius XM radio show "*Faith Based Investing*" on Channel 131. Or, you may have heard my radio commercials, or even seen me on local television, and possibly know me by the name "*The Investment Preacher*". Still, some of you may not know me at all. But no matter what has brought you here, *Welcome* and *Thank You!*

In addition to being an ordained minister and Senior Pastor of a church, I have also served an Investment Advisor Representative for the past 10 years. In my experience, I can tell you that Christians today are not aware of what their money is helping support when they make investments. In fact, most everyone just trusts their financial advisor to invest it for them and that is basically as far as it ever goes.

After attending a conference in 2019 in Dallas, TX, I began to learn that Christian's money (including pastors), are actually supporting abortions, planned parenthood, alternative lifestyles, buying baby parts from aborted babies, and other anti-Biblical, anti-family agendas.

Even Pastors who preach from pulpit that they are pro- life and encourage their congregation to be pro-life based on God's Word and yet, have their own investments such as 403(b), 401(k), IRA's,

Roth IRA's, and general investment accounts supporting principles that are against biblical teachings.

To be fair to the Christians and Pastors they aren't doing it willingly, they are doing it out of ignorance. In the pages that follow I am going to show you how you can identify where your money is going and what your money is supporting in your investment accounts.

Due to being an Investment Advisor Representative and an ordained minister, my intention for this book is to serve as your Faith Based Investment Coach. I not only want to point out the knowledge of the Bible but teach you how to apply it with practical application so that you can watch God bless your investments beyond what you can think or imagine.

Our God is a good God and He loves us regardless of our flaws. However, His Word tells us in Proverbs 23:12;

> ## Apply your heart to instruction,
> ## And your ears to words of knowledge.

In this book I am going to give you helpful instruction to open your eyes and give you knowledge of how Christians are being innocently and unknowingly mislead.

Grab yourself a cup of tea, coffee, or glass of water and get ready to learn something that I promise, you have never heard preached from most pulpits before. The verse of scripture that inspired me to write this book is Proverbs 24:3-4;

> *Through wisdom a house is built,*
> *and by understanding it is established;*
> *By knowledge the rooms are filled*
> *with all precious and pleasant riches.*

I want what God wants. Your rooms being, your investment accounts flourishing. Your 401(k), IRA, 403(b), or brokerage accounts. In the pages to follow are "7 Biblical Rules" that if you will follow, I believe God will fill your rooms with all precious and pleasant riches.

May God Bless You,

**D. Anthony Wright**

# BIBLICALLY RESPONSIBLE INVESTING—BEGINS WITH A "HEART ATTITUDE"

Do you believe that God owns everything and that you have been entrusted by God with the financial resources you have?

If yes, do you believe it is your responsibility to steward those resources in the manner God would find befitting?

# INVESTING WITH A PURPOSE

There is more to investing than merely chasing a rate of return.

When you invest in any company, you become an owner and help support (financially) the mission and vision of that company—the problem is that some companies are supporting ideals that are contrary to biblically-based beliefs (such as abortion, pornography, and/or human rights).

We created a better way of investing that combines your financial goals with a scripturally-sound investment approach.

## CHAPTER 1

*Rule # 1*

# WE MUST EMBRACE KNOWLEDGE

<u>My people are destroyed for lack of knowledge:</u> because thou hast rejected knowledge, I will also reject thee, that thou shalt be no priest to me: seeing thou hast forgotten the law of thy God, I will also forget thy children.

**Hosea 4:6 (KJV)**

Let me start out by saying first and foremost that the message of Faith Based Investing is not a condemnation message. The Bible says that "there is now therefore, no condemnation to them which are in Christ Jesus…" (Romans 8:1KJV) God is love. You will never do anything to make Him mad at you. In fact, we all mess up but thank God for His grace and that all we have to do is repent and receive His forgiveness and His mercy. As the Scripture states, it is lack of knowledge that we are destroyed.

Years ago, as a young boy growing up, I was always taught as most of you were too, to always be teachable and listen to my elders and my teachers because knowledge would take me where I wanted to go in life. It is important that we keep and maintain that mindset, even as we age, we must remain teachable and be hungry to gain more knowledge so that we may become the very best that God wants us to be.

When it comes to investing our resources that God has so richly blessed us with, it is important that we gain as much knowledge as we can and be good stewards of God's money.

As I mentioned in my introduction page, to be fair to Christians and Pastors they are not doing it willingly, but rather out of ignorance.

When I was fresh out of Bible College and taking the pastorate at my first church, one of my spiritual fathers told me, "Anthony, you can fix ignorance with education, but you will never be able to fix stupid, so focus on educating people with the Bible and give them practical ways to apply it in their personal lives."

In the pages to follow I will show you a portfolio of an actual client that first came to my office believing he was invested in biblical stocks because the company that administers his investment plan told him they were a part of a biblical responsible organization and his stocks were clean from anything violating his moral principles.

Due to privacy I have removed my clients name so that no personal information is revealed. The companies listed in this report have reported all of this information and is therefore, public information.

Very few people ever take the time to check the public record of companies to which they invest. Let's be honest, who has the time to thumb through all of that stuff? That's what your financial advisor is supposed to do, right? Wrong! Most financial advisors don't want to take the time to thumb through your statements and screen your investments.

To be even more honest, most financial advisors don't even care. Sad but true, all they want is your money to manage so they make a commission or a fee on their assets under management.

That is what makes me different. Being an ordained minister and a financial advisor, I answer to God for what stocks I advise my clients to invest in. It isn't always about the return you make on your investment, although I am not suggesting you have to jeopardize any return on investment. You do however have a moral and biblical responsibility to be a good steward of God's money that He entrusts you with.

So how do we have the time to do it when other advisors don't? We use a sophisticated software that does it for us. Once I have a persons investment statement, I am then able to run it through a software screener that gives me a public record of where the companies you are invested in put their money.

Faith based investing does not mean that you have to settle for less than the market as a whole. Last year we had some Faith Based Investment clients make more of a return than the clients investing in secular companies. Why? Because God blesses our obedience to His Word.

The second thing you must understand is that not all financial advisors are the same. Some advisors telling you that they do biblical responsible investment advice are just simply advisors that pay a fee to an organization that gives them the permission to use their name and the term "Biblical Responsible Investing" or "BRI" for short.

They may be great advisors, (I am not questioning their integrity), just stating facts. Many pay an annual fee to belong to a fraternity like club.

These two things make me, the investment preacher different. I don't belong to a fraternity or club and pay an annual fee every year. I am an ordained minister and a licensed Investment Advisor Representative. I actually take the time to run every single company ticker symbol you are invested in, apply the Bible to your investment accounts, and then make sure they line up with what you are preaching, living and believing. Let's not just talk the talk, let's walk the walk.

I can't force people or make them move their investments to where will they line up with their moral, biblical beliefs, but I will put in the time and energy to expose the truth of what these companies are doing with your money. Then it is up to you after that.

You may be saying, oh preacher, come on man there are no clean companies anymore. Yes, there are! In fact, there are about 1,000 plus. And, you don't even have to give up any returns on your money. In fact, you may even earn a better rate of return because you are now invested and lined up with God's Holy Word.

On the next few pages you are going to see some very well-known companies, possibly you are invested in them or maybe you even do business with them in your everyday life.

Don't try and jump ahead of me in this book, I will explain in another chapter how the Bible deals with that issue and how we are expected as Christians to deal with that issue, so please be patient and complete the book.

I am going to show you an example of what you are going to see when you contact me and have me review your portfolio.

Remember at the beginning of the chapter I mentioned that I would start off by showing you a portfolio of an actual client that first came to my office thinking he was invested in biblical stocks because the company that administers his investment plan told him they were a part of a biblical responsible organization and his stocks were clean from anything violating his moral principles?

Once this individual saw this report I am about to share with you, he became emotional with tears in his eyes. After sharing the truth with him he made the decision to become a client and I moved his investments into good clean companies. Instead of him helping to fund abortions and alternative lifestyles, he is now invested in companies that drill water wells, build shelters for orphans, print and distribute Bibles, build churches, and feed and house widows.

Companies that are "faith based" bring hope to the hopeless, bring healing to those that are hurting, and feed those that are hungry. They will not be a part of anything to do with abortion, anti-family or anti-Bible. That's right, they are not anti-Christ. According to the Scripture, we are not to be lukewarm. We are either hot or cold. Therefore, if it is anti-God's Word, then it is anti-Christ.

Who is funding this anti-Christ, anti-Biblical movement? Christians! That is correct and not a misprint. The very people that are supposed to be like Christ are the ones funding due to lack of knowledge. Not anymore, I want you to help me take the wealth of the wicked and put it into the hands of the righteous, just like the Bible says will happen in the last days.

Now it's time to turn to the next page and see an actual portfolio. Remember, this could also be your invested dollars.

## Invesco QQQ Trust
QQQ, NDQ, QQQ

11 Greenway Plaza, Ste. 2500, Houston, TX, United States 77046

Total Offensive Dollars (all share classes):

### $59,537,877,000

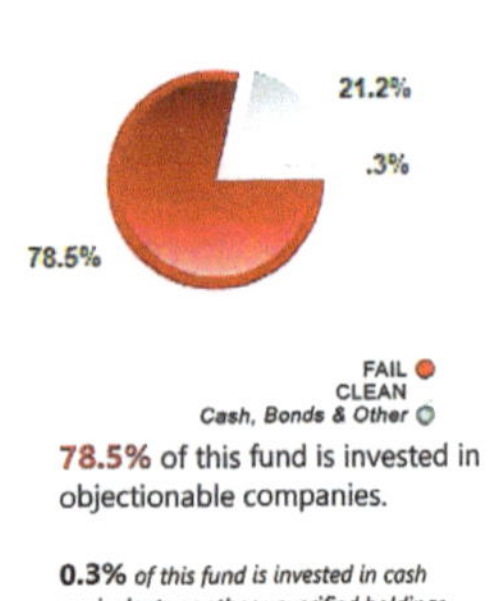


**78.5%** of this fund is invested in objectionable companies.

**0.3%** *of this fund is invested in cash equivalents or other unverified holdings. The values ranking for this fund could be understated or may change as portfolios fluctuate.*

**Large Growth**

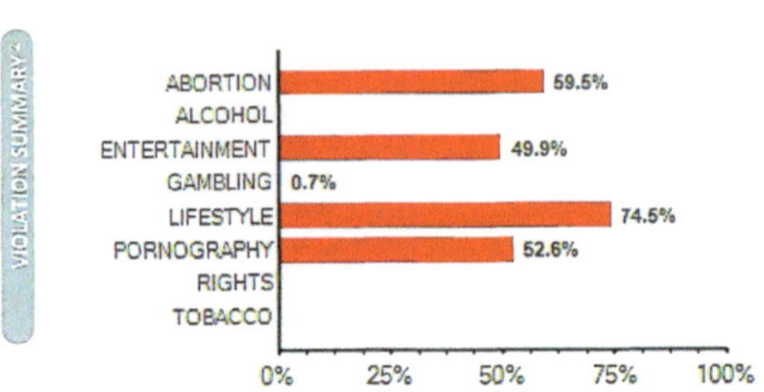


| Violating Companies | Ticker | % OF NET | | | | | | | | | |
|---|---|---|---|---|---|---|---|---|---|---|---|
| Microsoft Corp | MSFT | 11.12% | ● | ● | ● | ● | ○ | ○ | ○ | ○ | ○ |
| Apple Inc | AAPL | 10.72% | ● | ● | ● | ● | ○ | ○ | ○ | ○ | ○ |
| Amazon.com Inc | AMZN | 9.48% | ● | ● | ● | ● | ○ | ○ | ○ | ○ | ○ |
| Facebook Inc A | FB | 4.82% | ● | ● | ○ | ● | ○ | ○ | ○ | ○ | ○ |
| Alphabet Inc Class C | GOOG | 4.55% | ● | ● | ● | ● | ○ | ○ | ○ | ○ | ○ |
| Alphabet Inc A | GOOGL | 4.00% | ● | ● | ● | ● | ○ | ○ | ○ | ○ | ○ |
| Intel Corp | INTC | 2.73% | ○ | ○ | ○ | ● | ○ | ○ | ○ | ○ | ○ |
| Cisco Systems Inc | CSCO | 2.48% | ○ | ○ | ○ | ● | ○ | ○ | ○ | ○ | ○ |
| Comcast Corp Class A | CMCSA | 2.48% | ● | ● | ● | ● | ○ | ○ | ○ | ○ | ○ |
| PepsiCo Inc | PEP | 2.23% | ● | ○ | ○ | ● | ○ | ○ | ○ | ○ | ○ |
| Adobe Inc | ADBE | 1.63% | ● | ○ | ○ | ● | ○ | ○ | ○ | ○ | ○ |
| Netflix Inc | NFLX | 1.53% | ● | ● | ● | ● | ○ | ○ | ○ | ○ | ○ |
| PayPal Holdings Inc | PYPL | 1.48% | ○ | ○ | ○ | ● | ○ | ○ | ○ | ○ | ○ |
| Texas Instruments Inc | TXN | 1.42% | ○ | ○ | ○ | ● | ○ | ○ | ○ | ○ | ○ |
| Amgen Inc | AMGN | 1.41% | ○ | ○ | ○ | ● | ○ | ○ | ○ | ○ | ○ |

ABORTION
PORNOGRAPHY
ENTERTAINMENT
LIFESTYLE
RIGHTS
ALCOHOL
TOBACCO
GAMBLING

[1] *The pie chart represents each security and its percentage of net assets within the fund's portfolio. Totals may add up to over 100% due to rounding.*

[2] *The bar graph represents the collective corporate involvement in each individual screen. Screens are calculated independently and not based on assets, therefore totals will not add to 100%.*

[3] *Mutual funds are actively managed and the portfolio holdings are subject to change.*

*Investors are encouraged to consider the investment objectives, risks, and charges and expenses of an investment company carefully before investing in that company. A prospectus is available from mutual funds that contains that and other more complete, important information. Please carefully read the prospectus for any fund you are considering. You may receive a prospectus from the fund or from your financial representative.*

Are you shocked? His Financial Advisor told him because he was in an investment called the Invesco QQQ Trust that he was safe from anti-Biblical investments. The stock screener shows differently as you can see. Just by taking the time to screen his stocks he found that 78.5% of his funds were being invested dirty.

You can see it for yourself as this is all public information. Our software did the work for us. Once we input the stock or fund symbols, we found the truth. Look at where the fund spent 78.5% of their money. Abortions, entertainment, pornography and lifestyle. This is sad.

Just in that one fund, Companies worth close to $47 billion dollars were supporting anti-Christ and anti-Biblical things. Now do you see how we as Christians can impact the world for God just with simple knowledge on knowing where and what our money is funding? What if we ran that screener on 100 funds and found the same dirty money but moved that money over to Christian companies that supported printing bibles, built churches, fed the widows and orphans, etc. Good companies that took care of the hopeless, hurting and the hungry?

What I haven't told you is this person is a minister in their local community and pastors a church of several hundred people. They were embarrassed to find out that the very thing they are preaching against in the pulpit is the very thing they are funding with their investment money. This person said move my money immediately and get me into companies that don't fund things against my spiritual beliefs. They said, "I feel like such a hypocrite."

This is happening all across America and this is just rule number one. Now hopefully you understand why God tells us in His Word that we as His people are perishing due to lack of knowledge.

We can change that by being open to the truth and receiving knowledge so don't give up now. Join me for six more biblical rules to Faith Based Investing.

## CHAPTER 2

*Rule # 2*

# WHERE YOUR TREASURE IS THERE IS YOUR HEART

Lay not up for yourselves treasures upon earth, where moth and rust doth corrupt, and where thieves break through and steal: But lay up for yourselves treasures in Heaven, where neither moth nor rust doth corrupt, and where thieves do not break through nor steal: For where your treasure is, there will your heart be also. The light of the body is the eye: if therefore thine eye be single, thy whole body shall be full of light. But if thine eye be evil, thy whole body shall be full of darkness. If therefore the light that is in thee be darkness, how great is that darkness! No man can serve two masters: for either he will hate the one, and love the other; or else he will hold to the one, and despise the other. Ye cannot serve God and mammon.

**Matthew 6:19 -24 (KJV)**

This is one of my most favorite verses in the Bible. Where your treasure is, there will your heart be. Let that sink in for a moment. What you are invested in with your treasure, there is your heart. The theme of the rest of the chapter is how to find security for the future."

In the tough days and uncertainty of the world we live in, wouldn't it be nice to know that you have found security for your future? Guess what? You have. Just know where your money is at and what it is invested in. What are you helping support by being an owner of the companies you are invested in?

If you are invested in companies that are supporting things against God's Word and His principles, then your future might not be too bright. However, think how awesome it is to know that your future is not only bright but extremely bright and secure because God's blessing is on it.

Below is the "Believers Bible Commentary" of Matthew 6:19-24 passage:

> In verses 19-21 Jesus contravenes all human advice to provide for a financially secure future. When He says, "Do not lay up for yourselves treasures on earth," He is indicating that there is no security in material things. Any type of material treasure on earth can be either destroyed by elements of nature (moth or rust) or stolen by thieves. Jesus says that the only investments not

subject to loss are treasures in Heaven. This radical financial policy is based on the underlying principle that where your treasure is, there your heart will be also. If your money is in a safe-deposit box, then your heart and desire are also there. If your treasures are in Heaven, your interests will be centered there. This teaching forces us to decide if Jesus meant what He said. If He did, then we face the question, "What are we going to do with our earthly treasures?" If He didn't, then we face the question, "What are we going to do with our Bible?"

Ask yourself, is your earthly treasure invested in a company that funds anything against your faith, against the things of Heaven? Are your investments funding abortions, homosexuality, drugs, alcohol, pornography, etc.?

The answer is that you may not even know and that is why you need me to run your investments through our Faith Based Investing software. If your IRA, 403(b), 401(k), brokerage account, money market, Roth IRA, or any money invested in stocks that support earthly things then your treasure isn't going to be secure for the future. However, "If your treasures are in Heaven, your interests will be centered there. This teaching forces us to decide if Jesus meant what He said".

This one move and simple strategy will change your life now and secure your treasure and your money for the future.

*Rule # 3*

# WE MUST BE GOOD STEWARDS

And he said also unto his disciples, There was a certain rich man, which had a steward; and the same was accused unto him that he had wasted his goods. And he called him, and said unto him, How is it that I hear this of thee? Give an account of thy stewardship; for thou mayest be no longer steward. Then the steward said within himself, What shall I do? For my lord taketh away from me the stewardship: I cannot dig; to beg I am ashamed. I am resolved what to do, that, when I am put out of the stewardship, they may receive me into their houses.

So he called every one of his lord's debtors unto him, and said unto the first, How much owest thou unto my lord? And he said, An hundred measures of oil. And he said unto him, Take thy bill, and sit down quickly, and write fifty. Then said he to another, And how much owest thou? And he said, An hundred measures of wheat. And he said unto him, Take thy bill, and write fourscore. And the lord commended the unjust steward, because he had done wisely: for the children of this world are in their generation wiser than the children of light. And I say unto you, Make to yourselves friends of the mammon of unrighteousness; that, when ye fail, they may receive you into everlasting habitations. He that is faithful in that which is least is faithful also in much: and he that is unjust in the least is unjust also in much.

<u>If therefore ye have not been faithful in the unrighteous mammon, who will commit to your trust the true riches?</u>

And if ye have not been faithful in that which is another man's, who shall give you that which is your own? No servant can serve two masters: for either he will hate the one, and love the other; or else he will hold to the one, and despise the other. Ye cannot serve God and mammon.

Luke 16:1-13 (KJV)

Let's begin with the Believer's Bible Commentary interpretation of this passage:

The Lord Jesus now turns from the Pharisees and scribes to His disciples with a lesson on stewardship. This paragraph is admittedly one of the most difficult in Luke. The reason for the difficulty is that the story of the unjust steward seems to commend dishonesty. We shall see that this is not the case, however, as we proceed. The rich man in this story pictures God Himself. A steward is one who is entrusted with the management of another person's property. As far as this story is concerned, any disciple of the Lord is also a steward. This particular steward was accused of embezzling his employer's funds. He was called to account and notified that he was being dismissed.

**16:3-6** The steward did some fast thinking. He realized that he must provide for his future. Yet he was too old to engage in hard physical labor, and he was too proud to beg (though not too proud to steal). How then could he provide for his social security? He hit upon a scheme by which he could win friends who would show kindness to him when he was in need.

The scheme was this: He went to one of his employer's customers and asked how much he owed. When the customer said a hundred measures of oil, the steward told him to pay for fifty and the account would be considered closed.

**16:7** Another customer owed a hundred measures of wheat. The steward told him to pay for eighty, and he would mark the invoice "Paid."

**16:8** The shocking part of the story occurs when the master commended the unjust steward for acting shrewdly. Why would anyone approve of such dishonesty? What the steward did was unjust. The following verses show that the steward was not at all commended for his crookedness, but rather for his foresight. He had acted prudently. He looked to the future and made provision for it. He sacrificed present gain for future reward. In applying this to our own lives, we must be very clear on this point, however; the future of the child of God is not on this earth but in Heaven. Just as the steward took steps to insure that he would have friends during his retirement here below, so the Christian should use his Master's goods in such a way as to insure a welcoming party when he gets to Heaven.

The Lord said, "The sons of this world are more shrewd in their generation than the sons of light." This means that ungodly, unregenerate men show more wisdom in providing for their future in this world than true believers show in laying up treasures in Heaven.

**16:9** We should make friends for ourselves by means of unrighteous mammon. That is, we should use money and other material things in such a way as to win souls for Christ and thus form friendships that will endure throughout eternity. Pierson stated it clearly:

*Money can be used to buy Bibles, books, tracts and thus, indirectly, the souls of men. Thus, what was material and temporal becomes immortal, becomes non-material, spiritual and eternal. Here is a man who has $100. He may spend it all on a banquet or an evening party, in which case the next day there is nothing to show for it. On the other hand, he invests in Bibles at $1.00 each. It buys a hundred copies of the Word of God. These he judiciously sows as seed of the kingdom, and that seed springs up into a harvest, not of Bibles but of souls. Out of the unrighteous, he has made immortal friends, who when he fails, receive him into everlasting habitations.*

This then is the teaching of our Lord. By the wise investment of material possessions, we can have part in the eternal blessing of men and women. We can make sure that when we arrive at the gates of Heaven, there will be a welcoming committee of those who were saved through our sacrificial giving and prayers. These people will thank us saying, "It was you who invited me here.

**16:10** If we are faithful in our stewardship of what is least (money), then we will be faithful in handling what is much (spiritual treasures). On the other hand, a man who is unrighteous in using the money which God has entrusted to him is unrighteous when bigger considerations are at stake. The relative unimportance of money is emphasized by the expression what is least.

**16:11** Anyone who is not honest in using unrighteous mammon for the Lord can scarcely expect Him to entrust true riches to him. Money is called unrighteous mammon. It is not basically evil in itself. But there probably wouldn't be any need for money if sin had not come into the world. And money is unrighteous because it is characteristically used for purposes other than the glory of God. It is contrasted here with true riches. The value of money is uncertain and temporary; the value of spiritual realities is fixed and eternal.

**16:12** Verse 12 distinguishes between what is another's and what is your own. All that we have, our money, our time, our talents—belong to the Lord, and we are to use them for Him. That which is our own refers to rewards which we reap in this life and in the life to come as a result of our faithful service for Christ. If we have not been faithful in what is His, how can He give us what is our own?

**16:13** It is utterly impossible to live for things and for God at the same time. If we are mastered by money, we cannot really be serving the Lord. In order to accumulate wealth, we must devote our finest efforts to the task. In the very act of doing this we rob God of what is rightfully His. It is a matter of divided loyalty. Motives are mixed. Decisions are not impartial. Where our treasure is, there our heart is also. In the effort to gain wealth, we are serving mammon.

One of the top lessons about stewardship from this commentary is: "Just as the steward took steps to insure that he would have friends during his retirement, so the Christian should use his Master's goods in such a way as to ensure a welcoming party when he gets to Heaven".

As a Christian here on earth we should be concerned about being a good steward of God's money that He entrusts us with and in return we should invest our money into companies that insure us a welcoming party when we get to Heaven.

In the previous chapter I showed you a portion of the screener a Pastor that was helping support abortions and alternative lifestyles. Once I showed him where his money was being invested, he was a good steward and he had me move his investments to good solid clean companies. That is insuring a welcoming party when he gets to Heaven.

You may be asking yourself how many good companies are out there that do the right thing with our money that we invest? The answer is simple, well over 1,000 Companies are managed or ran by Christian boards, CEO's and CFO's that will only help promote good solid Christian, biblical things.

Due to the liberal news outlets and 47% of our country being liberal, we the general public don't hear a lot about those types of companies. If you want to be encouraged by reading about one such company with great Christian leadership, then go into any Hobby Lobby* store and buy Mr. David Green's biography, "Giving It All Away…And Getting It All Back Again" on how generously they use their profits to glorify God and build His kingdom here on earth.

Hobby Lobby was started in Mr. & Mrs. Green's garage. And today they have over 900 stores nationwide. I believe that is because of their faithful stewardship of the money God allows them to manage.

I know what you might be thinking. The Bible says in Matthew 5:35 that it rains on the just and the unjust. That is true. But remember that we are to lay up treasures in Heaven for our future. Let's invest our money in companies that do what is morally and ethically right and according our biblical beliefs.

*Hobby Lobby is not publically traded and is not an available investment option in any model offered.

*Rule # 4*

# WE MUST NOT BE UNEQUALLY YOKED TOGETHER

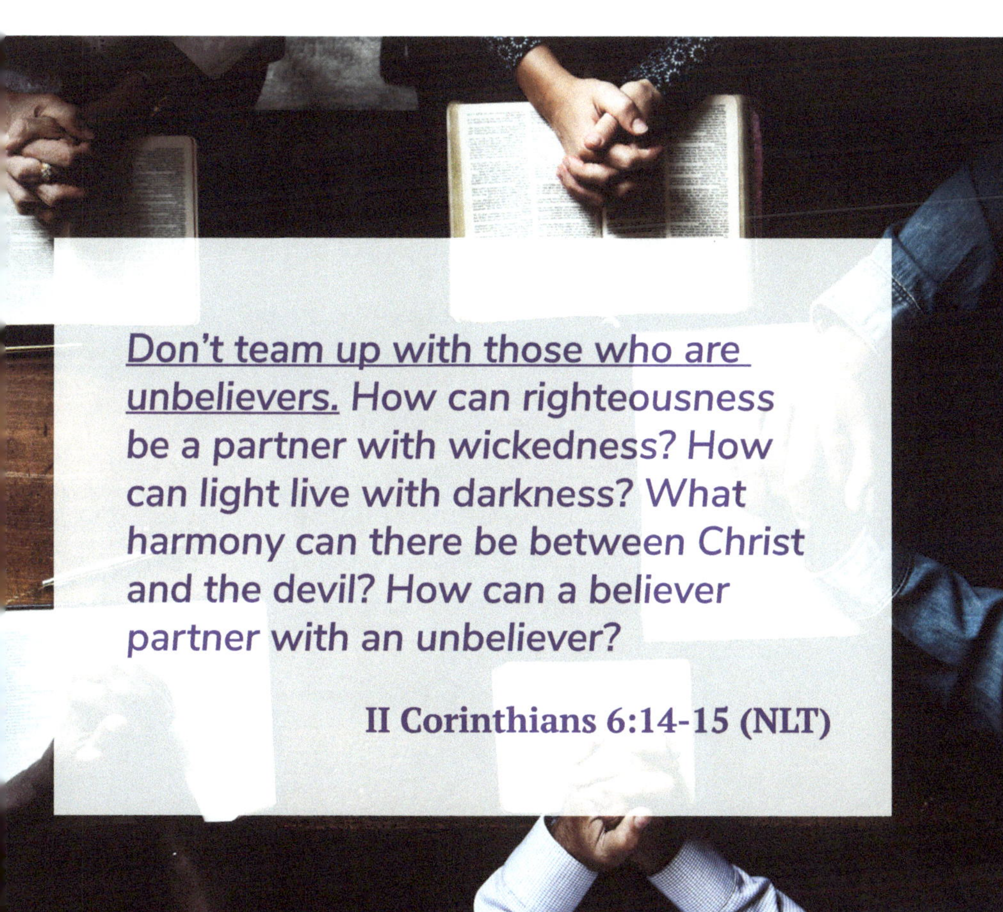

Let's continue with the Believer's Bible Commentary interpretation of this passage:

> Paul has told the saints to be open in their affections toward him. Now he explains that one way to do this is to separate from all forms of sin and unrighteousness. Doubtless he is thinking, in part, of false teachers who had invaded the assembly at Corinth.

> Mention of the unequal yoke suggests <u>Deu 22:10</u>: "You shall not plow with an ox and a donkey together." The ox was a clean animal and the donkey unclean, and their step and pull are unequal. By way of contrast, when believers are yoked with the Lord Jesus, they find that His yoke is easy and His burden is light (<u>Mat 11:29-30</u>).

> This section of 2 Corinthians is one of the key passages in all the word of God on the subject of separation.

> It is clear instruction that the believer should separate himself from **unbelievers**, iniquity, darkness, Belial, idols.

> It certainly refers to the marriage relationship. A Christian should not marry an unsaved person. However, in cases where a believer is *already* married to an unbeliever, this passage does not justify separation or divorce. God's will in such a case is that the marriage relationship should be maintained with a view to the eventual salvation of the unsaved member (<u>1Co 7:12-16</u>)

Additionally, this passage is also applicable to business. A Christian should not go into partnership with one who does not know the Lord. It applies clearly to secret orders or fraternities: How could one who is faithful to Christ consistently go on in an association where the name of the Lord Jesus is unwelcome?

Its application to social life would be as follows: A Christian should maintain contact with the unsaved in an effort to win them to Christ, but he should never engage in their sinful pleasures or in any of their activities in such a way as to lead them to think he is no different than they.

It's application to religious matters: A faithful follower of Christ would not want to hold membership in a church where unbelievers were knowingly admitted as members.

Verses 14 through 16 cover all the important relationships of life:

Righteousness and lawlessness describe the whole sphere of moral behavior. Light and darkness have to do with intelligence as to the things of God. Christ and Belial have to do with the realm of authority, in other words, the person or thing whom one acknowledges as master in his life. Believer and unbeliever have to do with the realm of faith. The temple of God and idols take in the whole subject of a person's worship.

Righteousness and **lawlessness** can have no fellowship together: they are moral opposites. Neither can light have **communion with darkness**. When **light** enters a room, the **darkness** is dispelled. Both cannot exist together at the same time.

**6:15** The name **Belial** means "worthlessness" or "wickedness." Here it is a name for the evil one. Can there ever be peace between **Christ** and Satan? Obviously not! Neither can there be fellowship between **a believer** and **an unbeliever**. To attempt it is treason against the Lord.

You are probably starting to figure out why I love the Believers Bible Commentary when I am preaching a message. I love in this case how it points out two things:

1.  "It is clear instruction that the believer should separate himself from **unbelievers**, iniquity, darkness, Belial, idols".

As I mentioned in chapter one, I would discuss the difference in being unequally yoked. Just because you shop at a certain store doesn't mean you are yoked with the leadership of the corporation or company.

The Bible says that when the Apostle Paul was in Rome he did as the Romans. It also says that we are in the world but not of the world. Therefore, by being in the world we have to shop at stores to buy groceries, toothpaste, paper towels, etc. That doesn't make us unequally yoked just because we "shop" there. We are living in a world that requires us to have certain necessities.

If we go into our garage to get in our car or truck, that doesn't make us an automobile. We are simply walking into our garage to get in our vehicle as a necessity to be mobile and have transportation.

In the investment world it is public knowledge that the local stores are there to promote and help the local community. They hire local workers, they pay taxes to the local city and county government, etc. The majority of the profits generated stay in that local community. Please go support the local businesses without feeling condemned of being unequally yoked.

When our children raise money for their school or sports team it is those local businesses that use their profits for that.

2.  "In addition, this passage also refers to business. A Christian should not go into partnership with one who does not know the Lord. It applies clearly to secret orders or fraternities: How could one who is faithful to Christ consistently go on in an association where the name of the Lord Jesus is unwelcome?"

Here is where Christians become unequally yoked with unbelievers concerning business. It is by becoming a stockholder. **Being a stockholder makes you an owner.** You become married into that Corporation or Company. The Bible is very clear "a Christian should not go into partnership with one who does not know the Lord". When our retirement accounts like a 401(k), IRA, 403(b), Roth IRA, Deferred Comp Plan, or just an investment account takes our money and invests it into companies that give philanthropy money, pays legal expenses, funds abortions, alternative lifestyles, pornography, sex trafficking, etc. **That makes you in partnership with someone promoting anti-Biblical, anti-Christ teachings.**

For those of you who are a current stockholder, or shareholder of company stock, you receive a proxy vote every year. When those reports are received via mail or email, 95% of the stockholders just trust the board of directors to make the best decision and rarely read what they are voting to do.

There is always a paragraph that say's this is what the board of directors have decided the corporation needs to do, please check the appropriate box that you agree or disagree.

The majority usually checks "agree". After all, who has time to read all of those pages? We trust the board of directors to run the company, right? In the illustration back in chapter one you would have just voted and agreed to support Companies that are supporting anti-Biblical activities; such as abortion, alternative lifestyle, pornography, etc.

Faith based investing is about not partnering (not about being unequally yoked) with these types of corporations. It's time to partner with corporations that vote yes to support the printing Bibles, digging water wells, feeding and housing orphans, widows, building churches, etc.

## CHAPTER 5

*Rule # 5*

# WE MUST NOT "LOVE" MONEY

For the <u>love of money</u> is the root of all evil: which while some coveted after, they have erred from the faith, and pierced themselves through with many sorrows.

I Timothy 6:10

Let's continue with the Believer's Bible Commentary interpretation of this passage:

> **6:10 The love of money is a root of all kinds of evil.** Not all evil in the universe springs from the **love of money**. But it is certainly one of the great sources of many varieties of evil. For instance, it leads to envy, strife, theft, dishonesty, intemperance, forgetfulness of God, selfishness, embezzlement, etc.
>
> It is not money in itself which is spoken of, but the love of money. Money might be used in the service of the Lord in a variety of ways where only good would result. But here it is the inordinate desire for **money** that leads to sin and shame.
>
> One particular evil of the love of money is now mentioned, that is, a wandering **from the** Christian **faith**. In their mad striving after gold, men neglect spiritual things, and it becomes difficult to tell whether they were ever really saved at all.
>
> Not only did they lose their grip on spiritual values, but they **pierced themselves through with many sorrows**. Think of the **sorrows** connected with the greed for riches! There is the tragedy of a wasted life. There is the sorrow of losing one's children to the world. There is the grief of seeing one's wealth vanish overnight. There is the fear of meeting God, either unsaved or at least empty-handed.

Bishop J. C. Ryle summarizes it this way:

> Money, in truth, is one of the most *unsatisfying* of possessions. It takes away some cares, no doubt; but it brings with it quite as many cares as it takes away. There is trouble in the getting of it. There is anxiety in the keeping of it. There are temptations in the use of it. There is guilt in the abuse of it. There is sorrow in the losing of it. There is perplexity in the disposing of it. Two-thirds of all the strifes, quarrels, and lawsuits in the world arise from one simple cause—money!

> The richest man in the world at one time owned oil wells, refineries, tankers, and pipelines; also hotels, a life insurance company, a finance company, and aircraft companies. But he surrounded his 700-acre estate with bodyguards, vicious dogs, steel bars, searchlights, bells, and sirens. In addition to being afraid of planes, ships, and crackpots, he feared disease, old age, helplessness, and death. He was lonely and gloomy and admitted that money could not buy happiness.

I love what Bishop Ryle says, "money could not buy happiness". That is such a true statement. Money alone cannot and will not buy you happiness. Happiness, peace and complete wholeness is only going to come from God and God alone. Having Jesus as the core center piece in your life is complete wholeness and happiness. It isn't wrong to have money, it is just wrong for money to have you.

How do you know if money has you? It is kind of like the list that Jeff Foxworthy put together back on his blue-collar comedy tour. "You might be a redneck if"… Money might have you instead of you having money. The list would be so long that I couldn't print a book big enough, so let's just continue by staying on the topic of investing. *"Your money might have you… if you only care about the return on your investment instead of what activities those companies or corporations are funding with your money."*

# TRUST IN THE LORD AND DEPART FROM EVIL

Trust in the LORD with all thine heart; and lean not unto thine own understanding. In all thy ways acknowledge him, and he shall direct thy paths. Be not wise in thine own eyes: fear the LORD, and depart from evil. It shall be health to thy navel, and marrow to thy bones. Honour the LORD with thy substance, and with the first fruits of all thine increase.

**Proverbs 3:5-9 (KJV)**

## Believer's Bible Commentary:

**3:5** First, there must be a full commitment of ourselves—spirit, soul, and body—**to the LORD**. We must trust Him not only for the salvation of our souls but also for the direction of our lives. It must be a commitment without reserve.

Next, there must be a healthy distrust of self, an acknowledgment that we do not know what is best for us, that we are not capable of guiding ourselves. Jeremiah expressed it pointedly: "O Lord,
I know the way of man is not in himself; it is not in man who walks to direct his own steps" (Jer 10:23).

**3:6** Finally, there must be an acknowledgment of the Lordship of Christ: **"In all your ways acknowledge Him."** Every area of our lives must be turned over to His control. We must have no will of our own, only a single pure desire to know His will and to do it.

If these conditions are met, the promise is that God **shall direct** our **paths**. He may do it through the Bible, through the advice of godly Christians, through the marvelous converging of circumstances, through the inward peace of the Spirit, or through a combination of these. But if we wait, He will make the guidance so clear that to refuse would be positive disobedience.

**3:7, 8** Conceit puts us on "hold" as far as divine guidance is concerned. When we **fear the LORD** and **depart from evil**, it means "all systems go." It spells **health to** the body and **strength** (lit. *drink* or *refreshment*) to the bones. Here again we are brought face to face with the close connection between man's moral and spiritual condition and his physical health.

It has been estimated that fear, sorrow, envy, resentment, hatred, guilt, and other emotional stresses account for over 60% of our illness. Add to that the terrible toll taken by alcohol (cirrhosis of the liver); tobacco (emphysema, cancer, heart disease); immorality (venereal diseases, AIDS). Then we realize that "he shall direct your paths" is more literally "he shall make your paths smooth" or "straight," but guidance is surely included in the promise. Solomon, by divine inspiration, was way ahead of his times in the field of medical science.

**3:9** One way in which we can **honor** the lordship of Christ is in our stewardship of **possessions**. All we have belongs to Him.

Please don't misunderstand what I am saying about being concerned with our ROI (return on investment). Of course we should be. That is the lesson that Jesus teaches us when describing the three men and their talents. The issue is that do we trust God by investing in correct investments? Do we buy stock in companies that support our Christian and Biblical beliefs and trust that in return God will bless the return on our investment?

I have clients who invest in both faith based investment models and some clients who insist their money is invested in so called "worldly stocks".

When I entered this business 10 years ago, I did not know that companies were funding such hypocrisy. At year end of 2019, my clients that were in solid faith based stocks largely outperformed the secular stocks. In the first quarter of 2020 when the Coronavirus hit our nation and the stock market collapsed over 40%, our faith based models were largely out of equities before the drop and were only down an average of 8%.

## CHAPTER 7

*Rule # 7*

# DON'T BE LUKEWARM

"I know your works, that you are neither cold nor hot. I could wish you were cold or hot. So then, <u>because you are lukewarm, and neither cold nor hot, I will vomit you out of My mouth</u>. Because you say, 'I am rich, have become wealthy, and have need of nothing'—and do not know that you are wretched, miserable, poor, blind, and naked.

**Revelation 3:15-17 (NKJ)**

Believer's Bible Commentary:

**3:15-17** The church at Laodicea was **neither cold nor hot**. It was sickeningly **lukewarm**. The Lord would have preferred it to have been extreme in its indifference or its zeal. But no—it was lukewarm enough to deceive people into thinking that it was a church of God, and so disgustingly **lukewarm** about divine things as to nauseate the Most High. Furthermore, the church was characterized by pride, ignorance, self-sufficiency, and complacency.

**3:18** The people were counseled **to buy from** the Lord **gold refined in the fire**. This may mean divine righteousness, which is bought without money or price (Isa 55:1) but received as a gift through faith in the Lord Jesus. Or it may mean genuine faith, which when tested **in the fire**, results in praise, honor, and glory at the revelation of Jesus Christ (1Pe 1:7).

Also the people were counseled to buy **white garments**, that is, practical righteousness in everyday life. And they should **anoint** their **eyes with eye salve**, that is, gain true spiritual vision through the enlightenment of the Holy Spirit. This counsel was especially appropriate, since Laodicea was known as a center for banking, textiles, and medicines—especially eye salve.

This verse and commentary pretty much says it like it is and there isn't much more to say other than don't get caught being lukewarm.

I strongly encourage you to not be lukewarm. From one Christian to another let's be on fire for God and get our investments lined up with His Word. I believe that you will see His blessings grow your investment accounts beyond what you can think or imagine.

> *Ephesians 3:20-21—Now unto him that is able to do exceeding abundantly above all that we ask or think, according to the power that worketh in us, Until him be glory in the Church by Christ Jesus throughout all ages, world without end. Amen.*
> *John 8:32 says, And ye shall know the truth, and the truth shall make you free. (KJV)*

The 7 Biblical Rules to Faith Based Investing has given you the truth and now that you know the truth and assuming you want to be invested biblically here are the next steps you need to take.

How are you currently invested and what are you really helping to fund? It's fast and easy to run our faith based screener on your investments and the best news is once you've been screened you'll know exactly what you are funding.

To receive your investment screening of your portfolio:

> https://go.retirementspecialtygroup.com/bri-investing

Or call me at

> 931-RETIRED (931-738-4733)

I look forward to hearing from you. May God richly bless you.